Treasures

A Reading/Language Arts Program

Mc Graw Hill **Macmillan McGraw-Hill**

Contributors

Time Magazine, Accelerated Reader

RFB&D ⓥ
learning through listening

Students with print disabilities may be eligible to obtain an accessible, audio version of the pupil edition of this textbook. Please call Recording for the Blind & Dyslexic at 1-800-221-4792 for complete information.

A

The *McGraw-Hill* Companies

**Macmillan
McGraw-Hill**

Published by Macmillan/McGraw-Hill, of McGraw-Hill Education, a division of The McGraw-Hill Companies, Inc., Two Penn Plaza, New York, New York 10121.

Printed in the United States of America

ISBN-13: 978-0-02-198807-5/1, Bk. 4
ISBN-10: 0-02-198807-2/1, Bk. 4
4 5 6 7 8 9 (027/043) 11 10 09 08

Treasures

A Reading/Language Arts Program

Program Authors

Donald R. Bear
Janice A. Dole
Jana Echevarria
Jan E. Hasbrouck
Scott G. Paris
Timothy Shanahan
Josefina V. Tinajero

Macmillan
McGraw-Hill

Test Strategy: Think and Search

Talk About It

Pretend you are a bird. What would it be like?

LOG ON Find out more about birds at www.macmillanmh.com

BIRDS

Words to Know

sparkled

saw

opened

soon

every

any

floating

---

cl<u>o</u>s<u>e</u>

h<u>o</u>m<u>e</u>

Read to Find Out

Why is the lake a good place for the ducks?

Floating Home

Last spring, we drove to a lake close to home. The water **sparkled** in the sun.

We **saw** some ducks. One duck put its neck under the water. It **opened** its bill and ate a plant. **Soon every** duck on the lake was eating. They ate **any** plants and bugs they could get.

Then they stopped eating. They quacked to us. As we drove to our home, we saw the ducks **floating** to their homes.

Comprehension

Genre
An Informational Story gives facts about a topic.

Reread
Make Inferences
As you read, use your **Inference Chart.**

Text Clues	What You Know	Inferences

Read to Find Out
What kind of food do you think Pelican wants?

Pelican Was Hungry

by Jim Arnosky

Award Winning
Author
and
Illustrator

Pelican was hungry. He **opened** his bill wide and then closed it fast.

That is how a pelican says, "I am hungry."

Pelican looked down at the water. He **saw** something shaped like a fin in the water. Quick! He dove down fast to eat it up.

It was a dolphin's fin. A dolphin is
much too big for a pelican to eat. So
Pelican flew back up to his branch.

Pelican sat on his branch. He opened
his bill wide. Then he closed it fast.
He was still hungry.

Suddenly, he saw a little head pop
out of the waves. Quick! Pelican dove
down fast to eat it up.

It was a turtle. The turtle was much too big for a pelican to eat. The turtle dove in the water and swam away. Pelican still did not have **any** food.

He flew up and away on the wind.
He looked down. **Every** little wave
sparkled. **Soon** he saw something
floating on top of a wave. Quick!
Pelican dove down fast to eat it up.

It was a coconut. A coconut is much
too big for a pelican to eat. Pelican
poked it away with his bill. He still
did not have any food.

Pelican swam and rode on top of the waves. He opened his bill and closed it fast. He opened it and closed it again. He was very hungry.

He flew up on the wind and over the waves. He flew all the way back home to his branch.

Pelican looked down at the water.
He opened his bill wide and closed it
fast. He was very, very hungry.

He saw something shine and flash under
the water. He dove down fast.

It was a fish, and it was a good one!
It was not too big. It had no big bones
and fins that he could choke on.
Pelican flew back up to his branch
with the fish in his bill.

He let the fish slide down his neck.

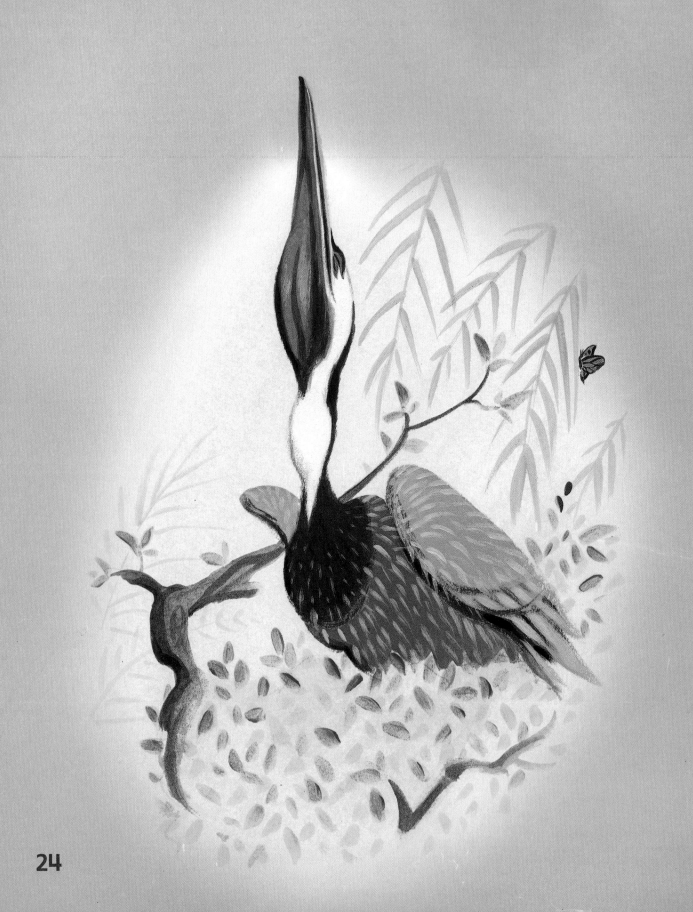

Then Pelican closed his bill and put it on his chest.

That is how a pelican says, "I am not hungry anymore."

Zoom in on Jim Arnosky

Jim Arnosky has always loved looking at plants and animals. As a child, he drew cartoons of animals. Today, his drawings show how plants and animals really look. He hopes that after reading his books, children will look carefully at nature and make their own discoveries.

Other books by Jim Arnosky

LOG ON Find out more about Jim Arnosky at **www.macmillanmh.com**

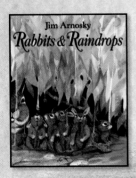

Author's Purpose

Jim Arnosky wanted to tell some facts about pelicans. Write about a bird you've seen. Tell some facts about it.

Comprehension Check

Retelling Cards

Retell the Story

Use the Retelling Cards
to retell the story.

Think and Compare

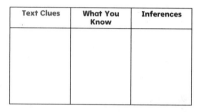

Text Clues	What You Know	Inferences

1. Why can't Pelican eat
   some of the things he
   sees in the water?

2. A pelican opens and closes its bill when
   it is hungry. What do you do when
   you're hungry?

3. How is a pelican different from other
   birds you know?

4. How is what Pelican eats different from
   what the ducks eat in
   "Floating Home"?

27

Poetry

Genre
Poetry often helps readers imagine unusual things.

Literary Element
Repetition is the way some words or sentences in a poem are used again and again.

LOG ON Find out more about birds at www.macmillanmh.com

Seagull

by Bobbi Katz

Seagull, seagull,
change places with me.
I would fly and glide
over the sea—
strong and wild and free!
My father would buy you a popsicle.
You could have my bicycle
And *all* my stuff – everything.
Seagull, seagull,
Change places with me!

Connect and Compare

How is the seagull like Pelican in *Pelican Was Hungry*? How is it different?

Writing

Was and *Were*

The verbs *was* and *were* tell about the past.

Write About a Bird

Jan wrote about why robins are special.

A robin is my favorite bird.

I was in Pine Park.

A robin was singing.

We were happy to hear it.

Your Turn

Write about your favorite bird.

Tell why it is special.

Writer's Checklist

 Did I tell why my bird is special?

 Did I use the verbs *was* or *were* to tell about the past?

 Do special names begin with capital letters?

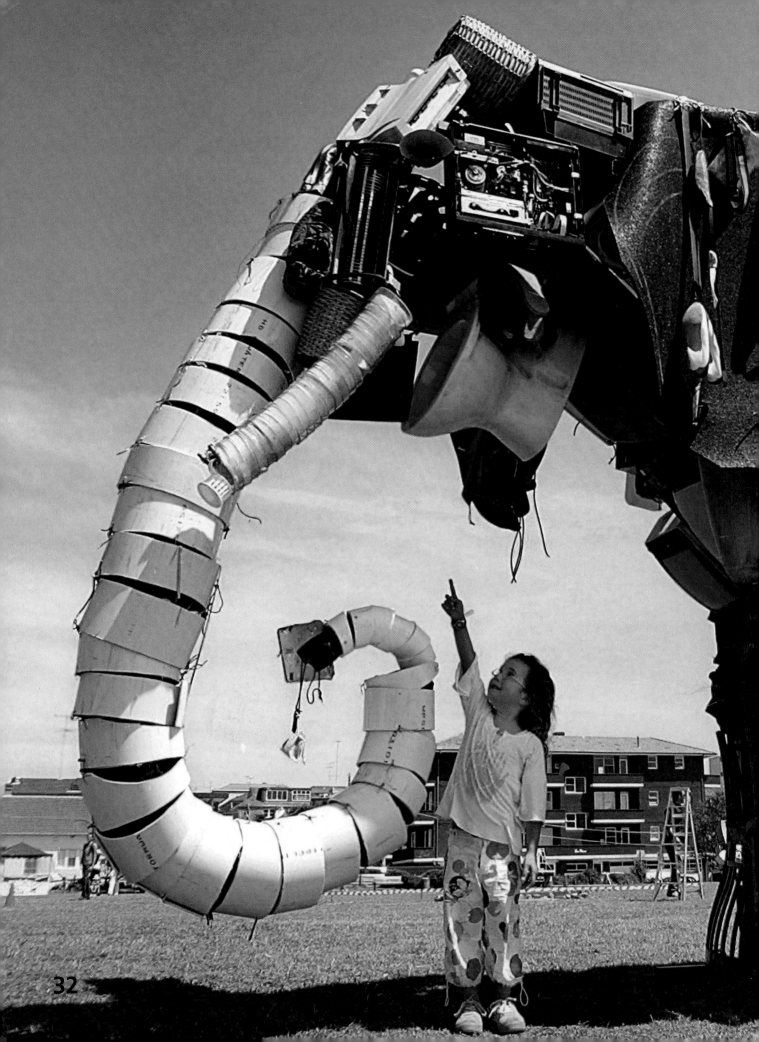

Talk About It

Why do people recycle things?

LOG ON Find out more about recycling at **www.macmillanmh.com**

RECYCLING

Words to Know

work
after
old
find
new
creation
done
terrific

_____

used
Luke

Read to Find Out

Why do Luke and his friends recycle old things?

Old Stuff, New Stuff, Used Stuff

Luke and his pals do good **work after** school. Today they are putting **old** cans and glass into bins. They **find** them at home, at school, and all over.

"This old stuff can be used to make a **new creation**," says Luke. "Old things can be used over and over again."

"That's why we bring them here," says Jill.

When the kids are **done**, Luke's mom says, "You kids did a **terrific** job. Now it's time to play."

Comprehension

Genre

A fantasy is a made-up story that could not happen in real life.

Reread

Draw Conclusions

As your read, use your **Conclusions Chart.**

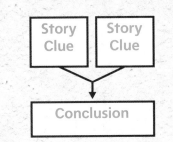

Story Clue	Story Clue

↓

Conclusion

Read to Find Out

Why does June Robot like old things?

Robot Cleans Up

Award Winning Illustrator

by Mary Anderson
illustrated by Michael Garland

37

June Robot liked to **find old** things.
Every day **after** school, she looked
for more old things.

"June, what will you do with all that
junk?" asked her little brother, Rob.

"I am going to use it," said June.

Today, Luke and his dad were bringing things to the dump.

"This is such good stuff!" said June. "I can use your old things."

"You can?" asked Luke.

"Yes," said June. "I have a plan."

June took Luke's old stuff home.

"June, is that more old stuff?" asked her mom.

"What will you do with that junk?" asked her dad.

"I am going to use it," said June.

June went to her room.

"Come and help me, Rob," she said.
"Hand me that tube of paste. I can
make a **new** toy for you to jump in."

Soon June was **done**.

"Get in, Rob," she said.

"June! Look at me jump!" said Rob.
"You make the best things."

"What is that noise?" asked Mom.

"What is going on up there?" asked Dad.

"Let's go find out," they said.

"Rob! What are you doing?" asked Mom.

"June! Look at this mess," said Dad.

"That's it!" said Mom and Dad together.
"There will be no more junk!"

"But this is all good stuff!" said June.
"Look! I made this for reading in bed."

"And she made this for me to play a
tune on!" said Rob.

"That is **terrific**," said Mom. "But this mess has to go!"

"Tomorrow, we bring the things you can't use to the dump," said Dad.

After Mom and Dad left, June looked
at her old stuff.

"Rob, I have a plan," said June. "I can have
a clean room and still keep my stuff."

"Can I help?" asked Rob.

June and Rob went to **work**.

"We can use so much of this stuff," said June.

"Mom and Dad are going to be so happy!" said Rob.

June and Rob worked and worked.

At last, they were done. June smiled.

"This is my best **creation** yet," she said.

"I'll get Mom and Dad," said Rob.

"Mom and Dad!" said Rob. "Look at what we made."

"What is it?" they asked.

"You'll see," said June. "I just have to pull down this switch."

"Your room is so clean!" said Mom.

"And you used so much old stuff," said Dad.

"Look!" said Rob. "This is the leftover stuff to bring to the dump."

"But June can make something new with it," said Mom and Dad.

"I can!" said June.

Who Made June Robot?

Mary Anderson says, "I am just like June Robot. I love to find old stuff. My home is filled with things that I have found and fixed up."

Michael Garland illustrates both his own and other people's stories. He paints and draws, and also uses the computer to make his pictures.

Other books by Michael Garland

My Cousin Katie
Michael Garland

CIRCUS GIRL MICHAEL GARLAND

LOG ON Find out more about Mary Anderson and Michael Garland at **www.macmillanmh.com**

Author's Purpose

Mary Anderson wanted to tell a story about an unusual machine. Write about a machine you'd like to make.

Comprehension Check

Retell the Story

Use the Retelling Cards to retell the story.

Retelling Cards

Think and Compare

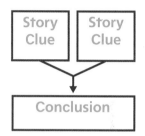

1. What do you think June's mom and dad will do the next time she brings junk home?

2. Would you like to have a friend like June? Why or why not?

3. June uses old stuff to make new things. How is this good for the environment?

4. How is what June does with junk like what Luke does in "Old Stuff, New Stuff, Used Stuff"?

Genre
Nonfiction gives information about a topic.

Text Feature
A Floor Plan is a drawing that shows where things are in a room.

Content Words
recycling
sort
plastic

LOG ON Find out more about recycling at www.macmillanmh.com

A Bottle Takes a Trip

Ahh! You just drank some water. Now you toss the bottle in a blue bin for **recycling**. What will happen to that bottle?

WE RECYCLE

A truck will come to pick your bottle up. It will go with many bottles to a recycling center.

When they get there, the bottles go down a big slide.

Now people **sort** the cans, bottles, and paper.

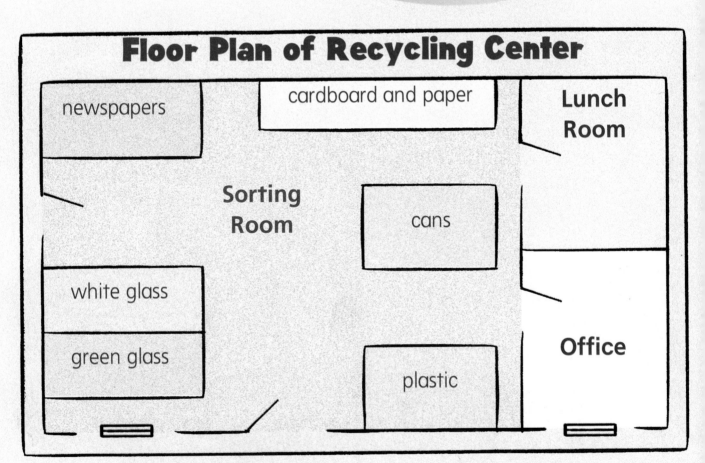

Floor Plan of Recycling Center

newspapers	cardboard and paper	Lunch Room

Sorting Room

cans

white glass

green glass

plastic

Office

Look at this floor plan of a recycling center. What kinds of things do you see being recycled?

Your bottle is made of **plastic**. It will
go to a factory. Here the bottles are
cut up into small bits.

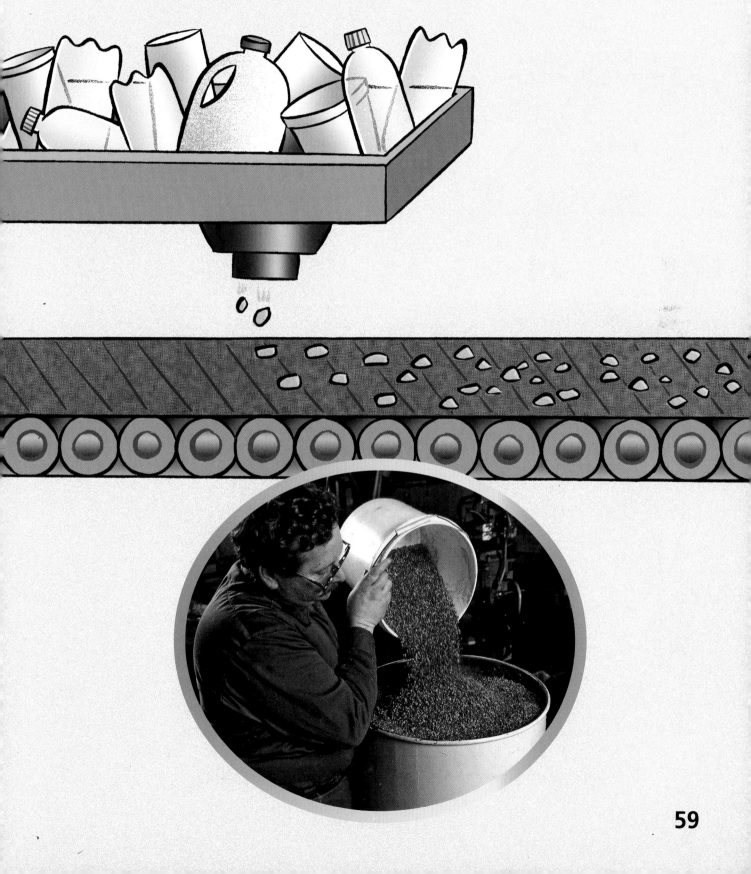

Next the plastic bits are melted until they are soft. The soft plastic can be used to make many new things.

The green rulers on this page were made from recycled plastic. Recycled plastic can also be made into yarn. It can be used to make socks and sweaters and to fill sleeping bags.

All of the things this girl has were made out of recycled plastic. One of them could have come from your bottle!

Connect and Compare

June recycles in *June Robot Cleans Up*. How is this like the recycling in "A Bottle Takes a Trip"?

Write an Ad

Carlos wrote an ad about recycling.

Do you have glass or paper?

Do you have plastic or cans?

Our *school* has recycling bins.

Use them! Save our Earth.

62

Your Turn

Think about why it is important to recycle.

Write an ad to tell others about recycling.

Writer's Checklist

 Does my first sentence get readers to pay attention?

 Did I use the verbs *has* or *have* to tell about now?

 Did I end questions with question marks?

Talk About It

What kinds of weather do you know about? What is your favorite kind of day?

LOG ON Find out more about the weather at **www.macmillanmh.com**

What's the Weather?

Words to Know

warm

sound

their

extreme

predict

cold

know

great

---

rain

play

Warm and Cold Days

What is this day like? It is **warm** and wet. The rain makes a good **sound**. Kids play in **their** homes.

This rain is **extreme**. But it will stop. Can you **predict** how the day will be then?

This day is **cold**. The kids **know** how to stay warm. They run and jump and have a lot of fun. What a **great** day to play!

How many kinds of storms do you know about?

There are many kinds of storms.
Which do you see where you live?

On some days, the sky is gray. That could mean a storm is on the way.

A gray sky can mean rainstorms. You may see **great** flashes of lightning. After that comes a loud **sound**. That is thunder. Time to go inside!

Lightning can make a tree explode.

Thunderstorms may have strong winds. The winds can blow branches off trees. Balls of ice may come down. This is called hail. It can hail when it is **warm** or **cold**.

Most hail is small. Some is bigger than a tennis ball. ▶

Some storms come when it is very cold. It can snow so much that you can't see. Strong winds can blow snow into big piles. This is called a blizzard.

A tornado can destroy buildings. ▶

Some storms have **extreme** winds. Tornadoes are made of very fast winds that spin. The winds can pick up trucks and homes.

Scientists have ways to **predict** when tornadoes will come. Then people can get out of **their** way.

Look outside today. Does it look like
a storm is on its way? Or is it a great
day to play?

Comprehension Check

Tell What You Learned

What did you learn about storms?

Think and Compare

1. How are a thunderstorm and a blizzard the same? How are they different?

2. Tell about a storm you have seen. How was it like the storms you just read about?

3. What would you do if you were caught in a blizzard, thunderstorm, or hailstorm?

4. How are the storms in "Stormy Weather" and "Warm and Cold Days" alike?

Test Strategy

Think and Search
Find the answer in more than one place.

Dangerous Storms

Some storms can be dangerous. Thunderstorms may bring lightning. Lightning looks like a great flash in the sky. It can be dangerous.

You are not safe from lightning outside. You are not safe under a tree.

Where will you be safe from lightning? You will be safe inside. The best thing to do is get inside fast!

Go On ▶

Directions: Answer the questions.

1. Which picture shows lightning?

◯　　　　　　◯　　　　　　◯

2. Why are thunderstorms dangerous?

◯ The rain will make you wet.

◯ The thunder is very loud.

◯ They bring lightning.

3. What should you do if you see lightning?

◯ Go inside.

◯ Stand under a tree.

◯ Play on the playground.

Tip
Keep reading to find the answer.

Write About the Weather

Rudy made a plan. Then he wrote a report about a tornado.

TORNADOES

A tornado is a very strong kind of storm. It looks like a spinning cloud. The top of a tornado is in the sky. The bottom touches the ground. Tornadoes are dangerous.

Your Writing Prompt

Choose a storm you've seen or heard about. Write a report about that storm.

Writer's Checklist

 Does my report have a main idea and details?

 Will readers understand my report?

 Did I check my report for mistakes?

What Scientists Do

Talk About It

What is a scientist? What kinds of questions do scientists ask?

 Find out more about what scientists do at **www.macmillanmh.com**

Words to Know

curious

idea

friends

kind

by

far

knew

house

———————

be<u>e</u>

d<u>ee</u>p

Read to Find Out

What makes the
seed look big?

82

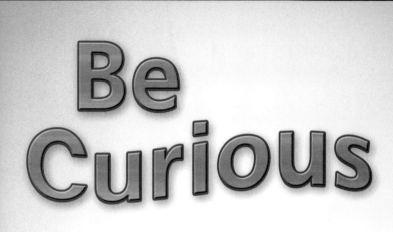

Be Curious

Are you **curious**? Do you like to look at things that are little? Then this **idea** is for you and your **friends**.

Fill a deep dish with water. Then, put something very little in your hand. Any **kind** of little thing will do. Put your hand **by** the back of the dish. Don't put it **far** away. Does the little thing look big now? I bet you **knew** it would. Do this with more things at your **house**. They will look big, too!

Comprehension

Genre

A **Biography** is the true story of a person's life.

Summarize

Make Inferences

As you read, use your **Inference Chart.**

Text Clues	What You Know	Inferences

Read to Find Out

What makes Ben Franklin a great American?

84

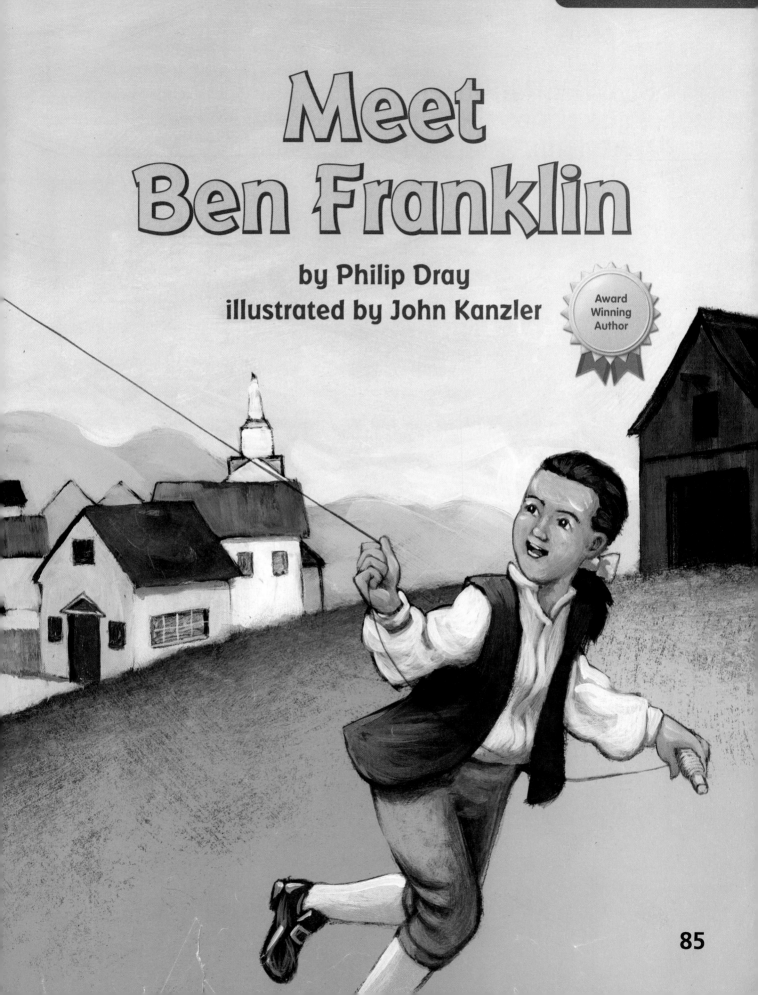

Meet Ben Franklin

by Philip Dray

illustrated by John Kanzler

Award Winning Author

Chapter 1

"Ben! Ben!" his **friends** called.

"Here I am," said Benjamin Franklin.

Ben was sitting on the docks. He was looking at the big ships. He liked the way the wind filled the sails.

Ben Franklin lived long ago. He liked to do many things. He liked to read. He was good at telling jokes and playing games.

Ben was a **curious** boy. He liked to dream. And he liked to make things.

One day, Ben made a red kite.

"This kite will be like the sails on the big ships," Ben said.

Soon after, Ben and his friends went for a swim. He had his new kite with him.

"What will you do with that?" his friends asked.

"You will see," said Ben.

Ben ran with the kite. The wind lifted
it. He jumped into the water and the
kite pulled him.

"Look at Ben go!" said his friends.

"How did Ben think of that?" they asked.

Chapter 2

Time went **by**. Ben grew up. He still liked to dream. He still liked to make things.

He made a new **kind** of stove. This new stove was little, but it gave off lots of heat.

Ben made a new kind of glasses. They helped people to see up close and **far** away.

"How did Ben think of that?" people asked.

When Ben lived, people did not know much about electricity.

Ben was curious about it. He **knew** it could make sparks. He sometimes saw the sparks when he put his key into a lock.

One day it was raining. Ben looked at a flash of lightning. It looked like a big spark. He wanted to know if that flash was electricity.

Chapter 3

"How can I find out if lightning is electricity?" Ben asked. "I can not go up in the sky."

Ben had an **idea**. A kite had helped him long ago. A kite could help him again.

"I can not get up there," he said. "But a kite can."

The next time it looked like rain, Ben
went out. He had a kite and an iron
key. He sent the kite up.

Lightning flashed. Ben felt the kite string shake. He saw sparks of electricity jump off the key.

"This shows that lightning is electricity!" said Ben.

Ben had an idea. He knew that if lightning struck a **house**, it could catch on fire. He put an iron rod on top of his house.

"Lightning will strike the iron rod, but not my house," Ben said. "The rod will keep my house safe."

Ben's friends put up iron rods, too.
Today we still put them on our
houses so they will be safe.

Ben was glad that the lightning rods helped people. In his life, Ben Franklin did many things to help people. He had more things to dream about and more things to make.

Meet Philip Dray

Philip Dray says, "I write books about Americans who do brave things to make our country better. I wanted to tell the story of Ben Franklin and his kite because he had the courage to try something no one had ever tried before."

LOG ON Find out more about Philip Dray at **www.macmillanmh.com**

Author's Purpose

Philip Dray wanted to write a true story about Ben Franklin and his new ideas. Write about one of Ben's inventions. Tell how it made life better.

Comprehension Check

Retell the Selection

Use the Retelling Cards to retell the selection.

Retelling Cards

Think and Compare

Text Clues	What You Know	Inferences

1. What kind of friend do you think Ben Franklin would be? Tell why.

2. What things in your home use electricity?

3. Why do you think Ben Franklin is a famous and honored American?

4. What did you learn to do in "Be Curious"? How is it like what Ben Franklin did?

Science

Genre
Nonfiction gives information about a topic.

Text Feature
Bold Print points out important words.

Content Words
scientists
microscope
photographs

Find out more about what scientists do at **www.macmillanmh.com**

A Close Look

How do **scientists** see little things up close? They look through a **microscope.** That makes little things look big.

Look at the **photograph** in the circle.
It was taken with a microscope.
It shows things you see every day.
Can you tell what it is?

This is **salt**. Now you can see the
shape of every grain.

This is **hair**. You have
about 100,000 hairs on
your head. Each hair has
a hard coating.

This is a blade of **grass**.
Sharp edges help keep
away bugs.

What else would you like to see close up?
What do you think it would look like?

Connect and Compare

What could young Ben Franklin have done with
a microscope?

Writing

See and Saw

The verb *see* tells about now. The verb *saw* tells about the past.

Kevin wrote about one of Ben Franklin's inventions.

Ben invented a lightning rod.

He saw lightning burn a house.

He put an iron rod on his roof.

Lightning struck it and not the house.

Your Turn

Find out about one of Ben Franklin's inventions.

Write a report about it.

Writer's Checklist

 Did I tell what the invention was like?

 Did I use the verb *saw* to tell about the past?

 Does each statement end with a period?

Favorite
Stories

Talk About It

Do you have a favorite story? What do you like about it?

Find out more about favorite stories at www.macmillanmh.com

Words to Know

before
happen
began
told
heard
glared
haste
falls

---

hung**ry**
sil**ly**

STRATEGY SKILL

Read to Find Out

What happens to the tree?

Have You Heard This Silly Tale?

One day, Hen saw a tree that wasn't there **before**. "How could this **happen**?" she asked.

Then the tree **began** to speak.

"Hello, Hen. I am a tree," it **told** her.

"I have not **heard** a tree speak before," said Hen. She **glared** at the tree.

The tree began to shake its branches with **haste**. One big branch **falls**. Now Hen could see that the tree was a big, hungry fox.

"Silly fox," said Hen. "You can't trick me!"

113

Comprehension

Genre

A **Folk Tale** is a story that has been told for many years in different ways.

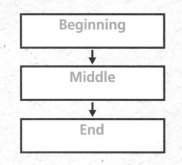

Summarize

Beginning, Middle, and End

As you read, use your **Beginning, Middle, and End Chart.**

Beginning

↓

Middle

↓

End

Read to Find Out

What happens to Little Rabbit in the folk tale?

114

Little Rabbit

A Tale from India

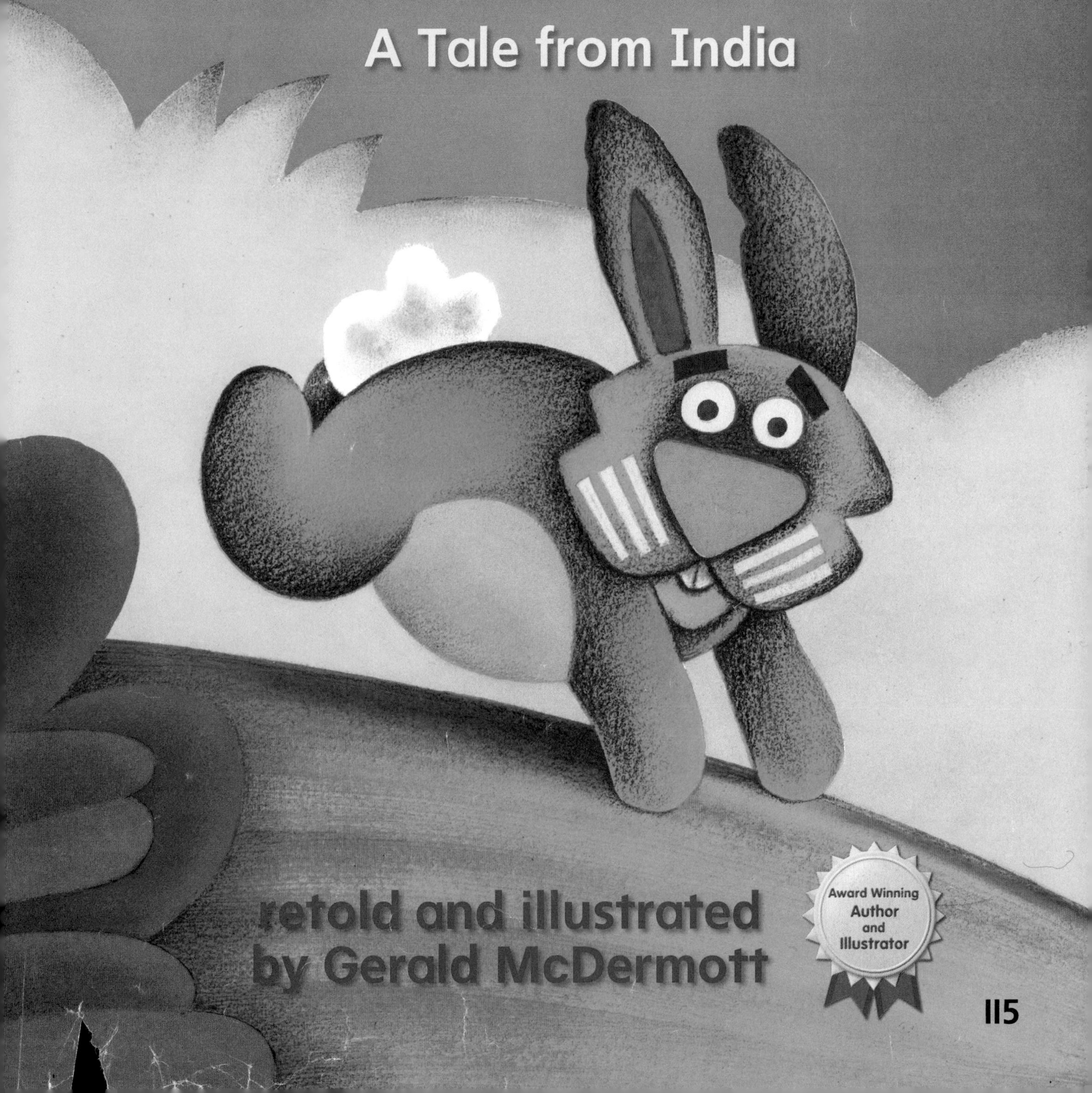

retold and illustrated
by Gerald McDermott

Award Winning
Author
and
Illustrator

115

One sunny day long ago, Little Rabbit was resting in the forest. He was feeling dreamy.

"I'm so happy," he said. "How good it is to be resting under this big, green tree."

Then he **began** to think. "What if the forest **falls**? What will **happen** to me?"

Just then, a banana fell from the tree.

The banana landed with a big thump. Little
Rabbit jumped up. He was upset.

"Oh no! The forest is falling," said Little
Rabbit. Then he ran away.

Little Rabbit ran as fast as he could. He ran on and on. Fox saw him running.

Fox asked, "Why are you running so fast Little Rabbit?"

"The forest is falling!" Little Rabbit called. "Let's go!"

When Fox **heard** that, he was very upset. He began to run as fast as he could. Little Rabbit and Fox ran on and on.

Deer saw them running.

"Why are you running so fast?" asked Deer.

"The forest is falling!" said Fox. "Hurry up!"

When Deer heard that, she ran as fast as she could.

Little Rabbit, Fox, and Deer ran on and on.

Ox saw them running.

"Why are you running so fast?" asked Ox.

"The forest is falling!" said Deer. "Make **haste**!"

When Ox heard that, he ran as fast as he could.

Little Rabbit, Fox, Deer, and Ox ran on and on.

Tiger saw them running.

"Why are you running so fast?" asked Tiger.

"The forest is falling!" said Ox. "Come on!"

When Tiger heard that, she ran as fast as she could.

Little Rabbit, Fox, Deer, Ox, and Tiger ran on and on.

Elephant saw them running.

"Why are you running so fast?" asked Elephant.

"The forest is falling!" said Tiger. "Get going!"

When Elephant heard that, she ran
as fast as she could.

Stomp! Stomp!

The whole forest could hear her.

Now Little Rabbit, Fox, Deer, Ox, Tiger, and Elephant ran.

As they ran they called out, "Run away! Run away! The forest is falling!"

As they ran past Lion, he called to them.
"Stop! Why are you all running so fast?"

"The forest is falling!" said Elephant.
"Let's move!"

"That is silly," said Lion. "Who said that?"

"Tiger **told** me," said Elephant.

"Ox told me," said Tiger.

"Deer told me," said Ox.

"Fox told me," said Deer.

"Little Rabbit told me," said Fox.

Lion **glared** down at Little Rabbit.

"Well," said Little Rabbit, "I was sitting under a tree and heard a big thump."

"Take me to that tree," said Lion.

They all went back to see the tree.

"Look!" said Lion. "It was just a banana that made that big thump. Next time, look **before** you run!"

"Thank you, I will," said Little Rabbit.

They were all sleepy, so they rested under the big, green tree.

Little Rabbit stretched. "I'm so happy," he said.

Then he began to think …

Gerald McDermott's Tale

Gerald McDermott retells and illustrates folk tales from countries around the world. Many of his stories are about animals that play tricks. He began to study art when he was just four years old! He likes to fill his pictures with bright colors.

Other books by Gerald McDermott

ANANSI THE SPIDER
by Gerald McDermott

ZOMO The Rabbit
A TRICKSTER TALE FROM WEST AFRICA
Gerald McDermott

LOG ON
Find out more about Gerald McDermott at **www.macmillanmh.com**

Author's Purpose

Gerald McDermott wanted to retell a folk tale. Write about one of your favorite stories. Tell the title. Explain who the main characters are and what they do.

Comprehension Check

Retell the Story

Use the Retelling Cards
to retell the story.

Retelling Cards

Think and Compare

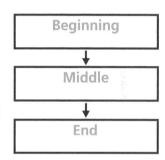

Beginning
↓
Middle
↓
End

1. What happens when Little Rabbit first rests under the tree?

2. Have you ever gotten a silly idea in your head like Little Rabbit did? What was it?

3. What lesson do Little Rabbit and the other animals learn? How can that lesson help people?

4. How are Little Rabbit and Hen in "Have You Heard This Silly Tale?" different?

Language Arts

Genre

A **Folk Tale** often teaches a lesson.

Literary Element

Repetition is the way some words or sentences in a story are used again and again.

Find out more about Favorite Stories at **www.macmillanmh.com**

Henny Penny

A Traditional Tale

One day, Henny Penny was looking for seeds. An acorn fell out of a tree and hit her on the head.

"Oh, my!" she said. "The sky is falling! I must tell the queen."

She ran down the lane. She passed Ducky Lucky.

"Where are you going, Henny Penny?" asked Ducky Lucky.

"The sky is falling! I must tell the queen," called Henny Penny.

"Oh, my! I'll go, too," said Ducky Lucky.
The two passed Turkey Lurkey.
"Where are you going?" he asked them.
"The sky is falling! We must tell the
queen," they called.
"Oh, my! I'll go, too," said Turkey Lurkey.

At last, the three saw the queen.

"The sky is falling!" said Henny Penny.

The queen picked up the acorn.

"It was just a little acorn," she said.

"Only rain falls from the sky. Go home and do not be afraid."

And so the happy friends set out for home.

Connect and Compare

How is "Henny Penny" like *Little Rabbit*? How is it different?

Contractions

A contraction is a short form of two words.

did + *not* → *didn't*

Write a Story

Chloe wrote about what Little Rabbit might do next.

Little Rabbit closed his eyes.

He didn't hear his friends.

He was scared so he opened

his eyes. All his friends were

asleep.

Your Turn

What do you think Little Rabbit might do next?

Write a story about it.

Writer's Checklist

 Did I use interesting words?

 Did I form contractions correctly?

 Did I use an apostrophe in place of an *o* in contractions with *not*?

Test Strategy

Think and Search
Look for the answer in more than one place.

How to Make a Paper Chain

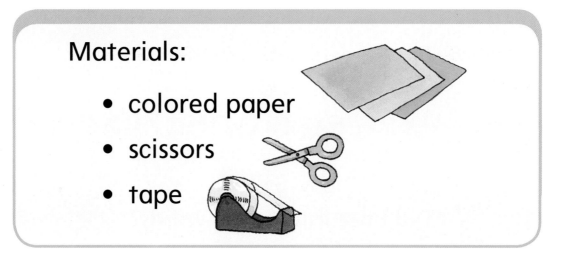

Materials:

- colored paper
- scissors
- tape

Go on

Steps:

1 Cut the paper into strips.

2 Take one strip and tape the ends together to make a circle.

3 Take a new strip. Put it through the circle you made.

4 Tape the ends of that strip together.

5 Tape more strips to the chain. Now hang up your chain!

Go on ▶ 141

Tip

Look for the answer in more than one place.

Directions:
Answer the questions.

1. Which one will you NOT need to make a paper chain?

○   ○   ○

2. What are the strips of paper used for?

○ to make circles

○ to make a picture

○ to write on

3. Why does Step 4 tell you to tape the strips?

○ to hang up your chain

○ to cover the holes in the paper

○ to make the circles in the chain

Go on ▶

Writing Prompt

What kinds of things do you like to make? Tell about something you made. Tell how you made it. Write four sentences.

STOP 143

Glossary

What is a Glossary?

A glossary can help you find the meanings of words. The words are listed in alphabetical order. You can look up a word and read it in a sentence. Sometimes there is a picture.

Sample Entry

Letter

F f

Main Entry

floating

Sentence

The ducks were **floating** on the pond.

Aa

after

After we ate, Scott washed the dishes.

any

Is there **any** more milk?

Bb

before

I wash my hands **before** I eat.

began

School **began** when the bell rang.

by
We like to sit **by** the fire.

Cc

cold
Ice is very **cold**.

creation
June's best **creation** was made from old things.

curious

I am **curious** about dinosaurs.

Dd

done

I put the cap on the glue when I am **done**.

Ee

every

I brush my teeth after **every** meal.

extreme

A snowstorm is one kind of **extreme** weather.

Ff

falls

Rain **falls** from the sky.

far

We went on a trip **far** from home last summer.

find

I was late for school because I couldn't **find** my book.

floating

The duck is **floating** on the pond.

friends

My **friends** and I play soccer.

Gg

glared

The cat **glared** at the dog.

great

We had a **great** time at the park.

Hh

happen

What will **happen** if you only eat candy?

haste

When Ms. Morgan saw the spider, she left the room in **haste**.

heard

Have you **heard** the story about the three pigs?

house

I live in a red **house**.

Ii

idea

It's a good **idea** to wear your seat belt.

Kk

kind

What **kind** of pizza do you like?

knew

I **knew** how to write my name when I was five.

know

Do you **know** how to whistle?

Mm

microscope

Matt can see things up close with this **microscope**.

Nn

new

I love my **new** shoes.

Oo

old

This radio is very **old**.

opened

This crocodile **opened** his mouth wide.

Pp

photographs

Kit used her camera to take **photographs** of the flowers.

plastic

I have a **plastic** lunch box.

predict

The weather person may **predict** snow.

Rr

recycling

Recycling helps save Earth.

Ss

saw

I **saw** the sun set last night.

scientists

The **scientists** are working hard to discover new things.

soon

We will be in second grade **soon**.

sort

You can **sort** your crayons by color.

sound

Thunder makes a loud **sound**.

sparkled

The fireworks **sparkled** in the sky.

Tt

terrific

Cindy did a **terrific** job on her project.

their

My neighbors have **their** own swing set.

told

Ms. Dunne **told** us a story.

Ww

warm

My new jacket is **warm**.

work

We **work** hard in school.

Acknowledgments

The publisher gratefully acknowledges permission to reprint the following copyrighted material:

"Seagull" by Bobbi Katz © 2001 by Bobbi Katz. Reprinted with permission of the author who controls all rights.

Book Cover, ANANSI THE SPIDER by Gerald McDermott. Copyright © 1972 by Landmark Production, Inc. Reprinted by permission of Henry Holt and Company, Inc.

Book Cover, CIRCUS GIRL by Michael Garland. Copyright © 1993 by Michael Garland. Used by permission of Dutton Children's Books, a division of Penguin Books USA Inc.

Book Cover, LITTLE LIONS by Jim Arnosky. Copyright © 1997 by Jim Arnosky. Used by permission of G. P. Putnam's Sons. All rights reserved.

Book Cover, MY COUSIN KATIE by Michael Garland. Copyright © 1989 by Michael Garland. Used by permission of Thomas Y. Crowell.

Book Cover, RABBITS & RAINDROPS by Jim Arnosky. Copyright © 1997 by Jim Arnosky. Used by permission of G. P. Putnam's Sons. All rights reserved.

Book Cover, ZOMO THE RABBIT by Gerald McDermott. Copyright © 1992 by Gerald McDermott. Used by permission of Harcourt Brace & Company.

ILLUSTRATION
Cover Illustration: Richard Cowdrey

10-25: Jim Arnosky. 28-29: Susan Saelig Gallagher. 30: Diane Paterson. 34-35: Kathi Ember. 36-53: Michael Garland. 56-60: Jessica Wolk Stanley. 67: Siede Preis/Photodisc/Getty Images, Inc. 84-101: John Kanzler. 112-113: Gerardo Suzan. 114-131: Gerald McDermott. 134-137: Diane Schoenbrun. 140-143: Anthony Lewis. 144-145: Carolyn Croll.

PHOTOGRAPHY
All Photographs are by Macmillan/McGraw Hill (MMH) except as noted below:

6-7: Theo Allofs/CORBIS. 7: (tr) Alan and Sandy Carey/Getty Images, Inc. 8-9: Studio Carlo Dani/Animals Animals/Earth Scenes. 26: Courtesy Jim Arnosky. 30: Digital Vision. 31: James Davis Photography/Alamy. 32-33: Torsten Blackwood/AFP/Getty Images, Inc. 33: Royalty-Free/CORBIS. 54: (cl) Courtesy Michael Garland; (tr) Courtesy Mary Anderson. 56: Ken Karp. 57: Javier Larrea/AGE Fotostock. 58: AP-Wide World Photos. 59: Richard Hutchings/Photo Edit Inc. 60: Richard Hutchings/Photo Edit Inc. 61: Ken Karp. 62: Artiga/Masterfile. 63: (t) The Image Bank/Getty Images, Inc. 64-65: Panoramic Images/Getty Images, Inc. 66: Derek Davies/Taxi/Getty Images, Inc. 67: AP-Wide World Photos. 68: Jim Cummins/Taxi/Getty Images, Inc. 69: Peter N. Fox/AGE Fotostock. 70: John Henshall/Alamy. 71: (tr),(inset) Jim Reed/Photo Researchers, Inc.; (c) Stockbyte/Getty Images, Inc. 72: AP-Wide World Photos. 73: CORBIS; (cr) Reuters/Jeff Mitchell/Newscom. 74: (cl) David Hanover/Stone/Getty Images, Inc.; (tr) Richard Hutchings/Photo Edit Inc. 74-75: (t) Randy Faris/CORBIS. 77: (tl) Joel Sartore/National Geographic Image Collection; (tr) CORBIS; (tc) Grafton Marshall Smith/CORBIS. 78: Comstock Images/Alamy. 79: (c),(cr) Dian Lofton for TFK; (bcr) C Squared Studios/Photodisc/Getty Images, Inc.; (br) Photodisc/Getty Images, Inc. 80-81: Jose Luis Pelaez, Inc./CORBIS. 81: (tr) Siede Preis/Getty Images, Inc. 105: (l) Andrew Syred/Science Photo Library/Photo Researchers, Inc.; (r) Davies & Starr/The Image Bank/Getty Images, Inc. 106: (t) VVG/Science Photo Library/Photo Researchers, Inc.; (b) Stephen Marks/The Image Bank/Getty Images, Inc. 107: (l) Dennis Kunkel/Phototake; (r) David Sacks/Taxi/Getty Images, Inc. 108: Banastock/Imagestate. 109: Philadelphia Museum of Art/CORBIS. 110-111: Paul Barton/CORBIS. 111: (tr) PhotoLink/Getty Images, Inc. 132: Courtesy Gerald McDermott. 138: Getty Images, Inc. 145: Getty Images, Inc. 146: Jennie Woodcock; Reflections Photolibrary/CORBIS. 147: (t) Photodisc Green/Getty Images, Inc.; (b) Marie Read/Animals Animals/Earth Scenes. 148: Layne Kennedy/CORBIS. 149: (t) Image Source/Getty Images, Inc.; (b) Timothy Shonnard/Stone/Getty Images, Inc. 150: (t) Getty Images, Inc.; (b) Tim Davis/CORBIS. 151: Jon Feingersh/CORBIS. 152: Joseph Sohm; ChromoSohm Inc./CORBIS. 153: (t) Ryan McVay/Getty Images, Inc.; (b) Photodisc/Getty Images, Inc. 154: (t) Royalty-Free/CORBIS; (b) Stockbyte/Picture Quest. 155: David Joel/Stone/Getty Images, Inc. 156: Dynamic Graphics Group/Creatas/Alamy. 157: (t) BananaStock/Alamy; (b) Masterfile. 186: Laura Dwight/Photo Edit Inc. 187: C Squared Studios/Photodisc Green/Getty Images, Inc. 217: Larime Photo/Dembinsky Photo Associates.